I0491643

Becoming Genius

PHILIP VAN HEUSEN

Becoming Genius

ISBN: **9798717447805**

PvH Publishers

DISCLAIMER

This book is not a book of psychology. The sole intent of this book is to motivate you to be the best you can be. This book should not replace any professional counseling you may be receiving. This book does not claim to bring you to mental health. This is just a book written for entertainment and education purposes. If you are having a psychological or medical issue, please go to a professional.

Becoming Genius

CONTENTS

Becoming Genius

THE SHOULDERS OF GIANTS

The only reason people become great is that they stand on the shoulders of giants from the past. Maybe this book will encourage you to stand on someone's shoulders and grow great yourself. Many have delved into this field and come up with great ideas. I desire to build on their work and encourage you to learn from them.

DEDICATION

This book is dedicated to Dennis Herendeen, Ph.D. He is kind and compassionate and he helps others without judging or condemnation. He makes people feel valued and important. He is one of the most understanding and likable psychologists I know. He works with difficult patients without judging them for their past. He is a joy to know and I am glad I have been able to spend some time with him.

1 *WHAT IS "GENIUS"?*

Genius Refers to More than IQ

There are several different ways of being a genius. There is the traditional thought that genius refers to someone of a high IQ. Someone who is extremely successful may be thought of as a business genius. Some think outside the box and come up with new ways of doing things. They too may be thought of as being a genius. The use of the word "genius" has come to be anyone who does something considered extra-ordinary.

Several people have studied what it takes to make a genius. Two of the most respected researchers in this field are Dr. Alfred A. Barrios and Earl Nightingale. While Earl Nightingale listed 25 characteristics of a genius, Alfred Barrios' research narrowed it down to 24. I am not too sure how much scientific research went into Nightingale's list of traits, but Barrios was a scientist and did his research to develop his list.

According to Merriam-Webster, a genius is

> **5** *plural usually* **geniuses** *a:* *a single strongly marked capacity or aptitude… had a genius for getting along with boys …— Mary Ross b: extraordinary intellectual power especially as manifested in creative activity c: a person endowed with extraordinary mental superiority especially: a person with a very high IQ.*

As said at the beginning of this chapter, "genius" has many meanings.

Let's be honest, you are interested in the traits that you can develop to awaken your personal genius. So, we will move on to the traits without further ado. Each chapter will be kept short to give you time to read the book then put the traits into practice.

2 *DRIVE*

Genius Is Hard Work

Trait number one might be obvious, but many start their journey towards greatness and genius with the mistaken idea that since they are smart, the journey will be easy. Even so-called natural geniuses must work hard in their field of expertise. Being a genius is not for sissies.

A note about hard work: Anyone who wants to be a genius needs to take care of their body so they can do the hard work involved. A sloppy diet will lead to a sloppy mind and body. Fuel your body correctly so that you will be able to endure the hard work involved in growing all the traits of being[i] a genius.

Drive says my goal is worth all the hard work and effort I put into achieving it. Once I have committed to becoming a genius, I will keep my eye on the goal and focus on achieving the goal. I will remember the fruit of my labor as a motivator to drive me to continue to work as hard as I can on the goal. I will not let anything turn me to the right or the left. I desire to finish my task and reach my goals.

If you know the story about Jacob, you might remember that he had to work seven long and hard years to earn the privilege of marrying Rachel.

> *18 And Jacob loved Rachel; and said, I will serve thee seven years for Rachel thy younger daughter. 19 And Laban said, It is better that I give her to thee, than that I should give her to another man: abide with me. 20 And Jacob served seven years for Rachel;* **and they seemed unto him but a few days, for the love he had to her** *[emphases mine] ...27 Fulfil her week, and we will give thee this also for the service which thou shalt serve with me yet seven other years. 28 And Jacob did so, and fulfilled her week: and he gave him Rachel his daughter to wife also. (Excerpts from* **Genesis 29:18-28***)*

Notice that Jacob said the seven years—which turned into fourteen years—was to him like just a few days. That means all the hard work was nothing compared to the reward that awaited him. He was willing to and gladly worked hard to achieve the reward of Rachel.

It takes hard work to become a genius and if you desire to become all you can be, you must be willing to put your whole self into the project. You must be willing to strain every muscle you have. You must be willing to work while others play. You must give the task all you have. Sweat, blood, and tears are strewn all along the path to the goal of becoming a genius in your own right.

Keep Your Eye on the Goal and Give Your All to Reach It!

Becoming Genius

Philip van Heusen

3 INTERNAL FORTITUDE

Nothing New Is Ever Accomplished without Courage

As stated in the last chapter, becoming a genius is not for sissies. It takes great courage for you will march to a different drum. You will do things differently than other people. You will be ridiculed for even thinking you can achieve your goals. You will be opposed. You may even become the butt of people's jokes. You must develop a very thick skin to survive and thrive. Remember that different is good.

Noah had courage. He had thick skin. He knew what he was doing was outside the box of mediocracy. He knew he would be made fun of. Can you hear the taunts hurled against him? "There is crazy old Noah. He thinks a flood is coming as the result of a terrible rainstorm. Crazy old coot." "Noah has gone crazy and way too fanatical with his worship. He thinks God has spoken to him directly and told him to build an ark. What is an ark anyway? All I know is he and his sons are building an awfully huge thing."

14

*8 But Noah found grace in the eyes of the LORD. ... 13 And God said unto Noah, The end of all flesh is come before me; for the earth is filled with violence through them; and, behold, I will destroy them with the earth. 14 Make thee an ark of gopher wood; rooms shalt thou make in the ark, and shalt pitch it within and without with pitch. 15 And this is the fashion which thou shalt make it of: The length of the ark shall be three hundred cubits, the breadth of it fifty cubits, and the height of it thirty cubits. 16 A window shalt thou make to the ark, and in a cubit shalt thou finish it above; and the door of the ark shalt thou set in the side thereof; with lower, second, and third stories shalt thou make it. 17 And, behold, I, even I, do bring a flood of waters upon the earth, to destroy all flesh, wherein is the breath of life, from under heaven; and every thing that is in the earth shall die. ... 22 Thus did Noah; according to all that God commanded him, so did he. (**Genesis 6:8, 13-17, 22**)*

It took courage for Noah to build an ark while all those around him were living lives of ease. It took courage for Noah to stand for the truth that God revealed to him and not to go the way of the crowd. It took courage for Noah to do his own thing. It takes great courage to draw outside the lines and think outside the box.

Do you have the courage to keep on keeping on when everyone is telling you it can't be done? Can you imagine Thomas Edison's assistant telling him, "But sir, you have already tried hundreds of filaments? Why don't you just give up and work on something else?" What if Edison had given up after trying the 900th filament?

(The actual number of Edison's attempts at perfecting the light bulb is a mystery but it is safe to say he tried at least 1000 types of filaments before he came upon the one he stuck with. Also, one needs to remember Edison did not invent the electric light bulb. That honor goes to an Englishman by the name of Humphry Davey. He invented the Electric Arc during the first decade of the nineteenth century many years before Edison's incandescent light bulb.)

Those who wish to be a genius have to become courageous. They have to be willing to walk alone. They have to be willing to go outside the box and attempt the impossible. Geniuses know it can be done even when it has never been done before.

Attempt the Impossible and You May Be Surprised to Learn It Is Possible!

4 DEVOTION TO GOALS

Devotion Keeps You Focused

Something that is devoted is totally given over to the object of devotion. If one is devoted to a spouse, that person's life revolves around the spouse. If one is devoted to their job, they do whatever it takes to competently give their all to their job. To be devoted means to give total dedication to the object of devotion. Nothing can severe you from what you are devoted to. Nothing can stand in the way of your devotion.

"Devotion" comes from the Latin word *"devovēre."* You might make more sense out of this if we use the past participle of this word which is *"devotus,"* which means to "be loyal to." Devotion is seen by loyalty. Loyalty indicates a dedication that cannot be taken away. According to Mirriam-Webster loyalty in connection to devotion "implies a faithfulness that is steadfast in the face of any temptation to renounce, desert, or betray."

A genius is committed by dedication and devotion to the cause. Your goals drive you to keep on keeping on. You do not in your devotion to achieve what others say cannot be done or just dream about doing.

In classical history, there were what were called "vestal virgins." These were women (usually) who had devoted themselves to serve the city's or country's pagan gods. In reality, they were temple prostitutes. They gave their whole lives to serve the gods as cult prostitutes. That is all they did. They did not have their individual lives to live for they lived solely and only to serve the gods.

While I vehemently disagree with that type of lifestyle and the slavery that was attached to it, I must applaud the devotion shown by their commitment.

Devotion often leads to advancement and recognition. People who are devoted to their job, often are the ones who are promoted. Devotion tends to lead one to success. Devotion to your goal of developing the traits of a genius will pay off with dividends of various types.

You may have seen the movie *Chariots of Fire* which portrays part of the life of Eric Liddell. When you take the time to learn about Eric's life you will learn he was a man fully devoted. He was devoted to two things: 1) God and 2) running. His devotion was in that order. His greatest and most important devotion was to God and serving Him. Next was his devotion to running. He felt his running was a way of serving God so in reality the two devotions were intertwined.

Eric's devotion helped him develop his peculiar style of running. It also led to his unbelievable speed.

He was invited to run in the 1924 Olympics that were to be held in Paris, France. He had spent his running career running the 100-meter race. However, in the Olympics, the heat for the 100-meter was on a Sunday. Remember, Eric was committed to serving the Lord. He refused to run the heat. He was allowed to run the 400-meter race instead. No one expected him to win. He was criticized and many tried to change his mind about running on Sunday and competing in a race he would most likely win.

He was devoted so no one could sway him to desert his devotion to his God and his principles. He stayed true to his course and ran the 400-meter. Believe it or not—since you are reading this book, chances are you will believe it for you know that devotion produces amazing results—he not only won the gold but he also broke the record.

His devotion paid off and he was hailed a hero. His story is so amazing that in 1981 a movie about this part of his life came to the big screen. For more amazing information, look up his life and read what he did after the Olympics and how he died in a prison camp held by the Japanese at the end of WWII.

Yes, devotion cannot be half-hearted. To be devoted takes you putting your whole heart and life into achieving the goal whatever it might be.

Devotion causes commitment. Commit to action. Commit to scheduling steps to achieve your goal. Have a plan to work on your goal daily. Make your goal your focus.

A final example of devotion is the pig and the chicken at breakfast. The pig is devoted while the chicken is glad to participate but not quite devoted. Remember to be devoted is to give our all to the task. Someone who is devoted is committed to giving their all.

The chicken drops by for breakfast and brings her eggs for the family. After giving her eggs, she happily goes off knowing she was a great help for breakfast. The pig, on the other hand, comes to breakfast to provide the bacon. The pig gives his all to breakfast and never walks off.

IT IS THE PIG THAT IS DEVOTED/COMMITTED!

Devotion Knows Nothing But the Object of the Devotion

5 KNOWLEDGE

Develop the Life-long Learning Habit

With all the gadgets that give us news and social trends, many have forgotten the pleasure and importance of reading. Read books in print, on Kindle, or some other e-reader. Personally, I prefer the feel of an actual print book in my hand and the smell of paper and ink from it.

As we will see when we look at the trait of curiosity, geniuses want to know about everything. They are constantly seeking new knowledge. They want to know "why," "what," "when," "how," and "where." They may not desire to become an expert in all fields, but they have a natural bent on learning about all fields.

I want to point out that "knowledge" and "wisdom" are not synonyms. "Knowledge" is the gathering of facts while "wisdom" is the ability to use that knowledge to the best benefit for all involved. "Wisdom" comes from God.

While man has a form for "wisdom," the best "wisdom" comes from God to teach us how to live according to His will and bring honor and glory to Him. Seek the wisdom from God and you will surpass the wisdom of this world.

Back to knowledge. Who wrote the book with the first line "Call me Ishmael"?[ii] Which book begins with "It was the best of times, it was the worse of times"?[iii] A genius is a well-read person. They read for enjoyment, enlightenment, knowledge, and inspiration. I wonder how many modern inventions are the result of someone reading and thinking, "I think we can make something like that," then making it.

Read and gather knowledge on a wide range of subjects. Don't be a narrow-reader spending time reading just your area of expertise. Read in as many areas as you can. Read non-fiction as well as fiction. Read the classics. Read updated research. Read!!!

I believe it was Cicero who said, "If you have a garden and a library, you have everything you need." I so identify with this quotation. I love my rose garden and my library is full of knowledge. I often tell my wife that "my books are my truest friends."

"The love of learning, the sequestered nooks, And all the sweet serenity of books"—Henry Wadsworth Longfellow

Erasmus felt that books and reading was so important that he said, "When I have a little money, I buy books; and if I have any left, I buy food and clothes." – Erasmus

Through books, I have been to places to which I could never afford to travel. I have seen things that I would never have seen in real life. I have visited sites of wonder. I have conversed with great men and women of the past. "That's the thing about books. They let you travel without moving your feet." – Jhumpa Lahiri in *The Namesake*.

Since the goal is to become extraordinary, this next quotation from Haruki Murakami is *apropos*. "If you only read the books that everyone else is reading, you can only think what everyone else is thinking." – in *Norwegian Wood*.

This country has seen a sharp decline in culture and ingenuity due to the lack of reading. It disturbs me to hear so many people say, "No, I have not read the book but I have seen the video." My friends, that is not the same. Develop the discipline of reading. "You don't have to burn books to destroy a culture. Just get people to stop reading them." – Ray Bradbury in *Fahrenheit 451*

"A room without books is like a body without a soul." – Cicero. Have a book in every room so it is easily accessible.

"One glance at a book and you hear the voice of another person, perhaps someone dead for 1,000 years. To read is to voyage through time." – Carl Sagan.

"Once you learn to read, you will be forever free." – Frederick Douglass. This is from a man who should know.

"The reading of all good books is like a conversation with the finest minds of past centuries." – Rene Descartes. You don't only learn from them, you are inspired by them, and you don't have to reinvent the wheel.

"You think your pain and your heartbreak are unprecedented in the history of the world, but then you read. It was books that taught me that the things that tormented me most were the very things that connected me with all the people who were alive, who had ever been alive." – James Baldwin. Often in this world, you feel you are the only one going through what you have to endure. Reading shows you that you are not alone.

"Reading is important. If you know how to read, then the whole world opens up to you." – Barack Obama

Have you read the classics? Everyone should read from the classics. If you have not read many or any of the classics, get busy reading them.

Read! READ!! And again I say, "READ!!!"

Learn by reading and by taking formal and/or informal classes. Attend workshops and panel discussions. Watch informational TV. Some places to find knowledge include:

➤ https://www.coursera.org/

➤ https://www.edx.org/

➤ https://www.openculture.com/freeonlinecourses

➤ https://www.openculture.com/freeonlinecourses

➤ https://online.stanford.edu/free-courses

➤ https://online-learning.harvard.edu/catalog/free

Many universities and colleges offer complete degrees online. You can earn from the AA/AS level to the Ph.D. level all online or with very little on-campus time. Some of the universities are excellent but some as diploma mills and should be avoided. Diploma mills usually require more money than time. □

Some colleges that offer online degrees are:

* ❖ https://www.apus.edu/

* ❖ https://www.liberty.edu/

* ❖ https://www.norwich.edu/

* ❖ https://www.snhu.edu/

* ❖ https://www.wgu.edu/

Abd the list goes on and on and on.

You are smart enough to do your research and find the courses and/or degree that matches your needs, desires, and likes.

Bottom line: Dedicate yourself to life-long learning!!

Commit to Never Going to Bed without Having Learned Something New During that Day.

Philip van Heusen

6 HONESTY

Speaking the truth in love. Ephesians 4:15

G eniuses are honest even to a fault. Honesty includes being straightforward. Honesty also includes being honest even about our mistakes and errors. Yes, geniuses are human too and as such are prone to making mistakes. Being honest also allows us to learn from our mistakes.

Let me tell you a story of when my honesty was rebuked because it was not considered socially correct. Yes, geniuses often struggle with social interaction and knowing what is and what is not socially acceptable. To this day, I am still not sure what I did wrong. I was honest and direct, but my honesty was not appreciated.

Years ago, I made my sister-in-law a tea box. It was very pretty and my wife and I filled it with tea bags, honey straws, and some Stevia. We met my brother and his wife at a nice restaurant and I proudly gave my hard work and effort to his wife. In my attempt at being honest, I said, "If you don's like the tea, it is ok. I can't stand that brand so we had some left and had gotten some at the motel. I thought I would give it to you in case you like that brand."

Trust me, it was not Twinings. It was another well-known brand of tea from England that I find disgusting. I was trying to be empathetic and let my sister-in-law know it was fine if she did not like it.

I was quickly told by my wife and my sister-in-law you don't tell the person you give a gift to that it might not taste good but that is ok. No compliment on the fine workmanship on the tea box. Just correction of my social misstep by being honest. I should have just given the tea and tea box and kept my mouth shut about my opinion of the tea. I thought I was being nice but socially it was not seen that way.

Yes, honesty is the best policy but sometimes we can say too much in our attempt at being honest. This was not the first time my honesty was not appreciated and I am sure it will not be the last.

Mark Twain said, "If you tell the truth, you don't have to remember anything." He means the truth stands by itself. If you lie, you have to remember that lie to keep it going. Too much emotional energy and brain drain for those who are seeking to be a genius to bother will. Honesty allows us to focus on what is important.

If people learn by observation of your lifestyle that you are honest, they learn they can trust what you say. If you say you are going to do something then always do it, they learn to believe what you say. Honesty builds both character and reputation. In all of your endeavors, BE HONEST!

Lying is one of the things God hates. He pounces on the lier with judgment. He hates lying because He is the Truth and in Him is nothing but the truth. Lies are opposed to truth.

Just some verses to show how much God values truth:

> *23 But the hour cometh, and now is, when the true worshippers shall worship the Father in spirit and in truth: for the Father seeketh such to worship him. 24 God is a Spirit: and they that worship him must worship him in spirit and in truth.* **(John 4:23-24)**

> *And ye shall know the truth, and the truth shall make you free.* **(John 8:32)**

> *Jesus saith unto him, I am the way, the truth, and the life: no man cometh unto the Father, but by me.* **(John 14:6)**

> *Sanctify them through thy truth: thy word is truth.* **(John 17:17)**

To be successful, we must live in truth. We must be completely honest in our dealings with others. We also must be brutely honest in our evaluation of ourselves. We must be able to look in the mirror and honestly critique ourselves. If we lie to ourselves, we will never amount to much. We must be honest about our weaknesses and our strengths.

I had a desire to become a brain surgeon. I thought about it long and hard. I love studying the working of the brain. Upon close and honest evaluation, I gave up on becoming a brain surgeon. You see, I had Sydenham Chorea as a child. As a result, I have had a residual tic that hits me at different times. I could just see myself in the middle of brain surgery and having a tic attack. One thing you never want to hear your brain surgeon say in the middle of brain surgery is "Oops!" I decided that brain surgery was not in my future.

Honesty means total honesty. Just because something is true does not mean you have to say it. Honesty says it will be honest but it does not preclude diplomacy. Honest realizes that the truth may hurt but in the long-range, it will help.

Honesty includes not stealing pencils from work, reporting all income on the tax forms, obeying the rules, and so much more.

Honest people tend to be the ones who get recognized and honored. Honest people are the ones who get the promotions. Being honest is just good living.

Be Honest No Matter What Others Are Doing!!

7 OPTIMISM

Optimism Needs to Be Tempered with Reality

Geniuses tend to be eternal optimists. They believe strongly that hope springs eternal. They believe the future will see their successes. They believe the fight is worth it. They see themselves becoming better and better. In their eyes, the future is bright and full of hope. They believe they will succeed.

They look out the window and see that it is raining. Then they say, "It is a beautiful day! The plants need the rain and ducks do well in this type of weather." They look on the bright-side of life. They seek to see the good in every situation and all people. They take a bad circumstance and determine to turn it into something good.

They, if they are Christian, wholly believe that God will work something good out of everything. They think the good and the bad work together to bring about the best.

28 And we know that all things work together for good to them that love God, to them who are the called according to his purpose. 29 For whom he did foreknow, he also did predestinate to be conformed to the image of his Son, that he might be the firstborn among many brethren. **(Romans 8:28-29)**

They do not believe in failure but they believe that so-called failures are just learning keys to know what won't work. They take "failures" in stride knowing they learn from them and develop new directions dictated by the "failure." I believe Edison commented that he did not fail hundreds of times but learned hundreds of ways his light would not work.

Optimism understands it is dark at night but they hold to the truth that the sun will rise in the morning. They don't look at the dark as a curse but as a chance to see the miracle of sunrise. They don't see how bleak a situation is but they see how great a change can be made in the situation.

Optimism is not blind. It is not ignorant. The person who said, "Ignorance is bliss" was not an optimist but a fool. Ignorance is not bliss but it is slavery and deadly.

Optimists tend to be realists too. They see the roadblock but realize they can make a detour and still come out at the goal. Realists see the problem and do not call it a problem, but call it an opportunity to do things differently. Optimists see the issue and think, there is a way to overcome this and reach my goal.

Optimists Don't Let a Little Thing Like a Roadblock Hinder Them in Pursuit of Their Goal!

8 ABILITY TO JUDGE

Look at Every Angle before Making a Judgment

Aah! The willingness to change your opinion! A closed mind is useless. It will not learn. It will not try new methods. It is closed to becoming a genius. Geniuses can and do see everything from many different angles and will change their mind when presented with new facts. Don't become too rigid.

Judging is not condemning. Judging is using discernment to decide among different options. Judging is necessary to make proper and right choices. Judging allows geniuses to look at all sides of a problem or situation and then make the correct choice. Judging is picking the proper path to follow. Judging saves time by keeping you from having to travel each path and waste time.

If you get to know me, you will learn I am a great lover of checklists, comparison boxes, and maps. To make good decisions takes good information and research. To decide between two or more options, learn as much as you can about each decision. This is easiest by using comparison methods.

List the traits or functions you need, then compare each of your options to the list. The one that is most favorable wins!

Use a pros and cons sheet. Take a sheet of paper and at the top write on one side Pros and then place on the other side Cons. Draw a line down the middle of the sheet and under the pros list all the pros for that item and under the cons list all the cons. If a choice has more cons than pros, junk it. When you narrow the choices down, compare each one to each other and see who has more cons. In this decision, also consider how strong each pro or con is.

Use a table to list all the possible choices and the desired components. List the choices on the rows and the components on the columns. Check the boxes on each row for the components the choices contain. Then pick the one that has the most components you consider important.

There are many other ways you can compare choices to help you judge which choice is best for you. Don't forget to get advice from others who know about the field you are trying to make your choices from. For instance, please don't ask me which engine part would be the best for you to use. I have very little (ok basically none) knowledge concerning the mechanics of a vehicle.

Seek advice from people who both know you and know the subject. Seek advice from people you consider wise and successful. Seek advice from those who have been in your shoes.

God says, "Where *there is* no counsel, the people fall; But in the multitude of counselors *there is* safety" (Proverbs 11:14, NKJV). In the same vein, He says, "Without counsel plans fail, but with many advisers they succeed (Proverbs 15:22, ESV). God advises we lean on wise counselors to make wise decisions.

You need to judge based on facts not feelings. Feelings are too easily deceived. Facts are what they are. They do not change on a whim. They do not change based on your mood. They do not change according to the winds of the times. Facts remain constant. The interpretation of facts might change, but the facts remain constant.

The death knell of making wise decisions is prejudging. Give all options a chance. Never, ever, even think of using the excuse—we never did it that way before.

Don't Prejudge Choices

9 ENTHUSIASM

Unless You Become Enthusiastic about Your Goal, You Will Not Reach It

E nthusiasm is an interesting word with even a more interesting etymology. Not to get too deep, but enthusiasm had to do with being inspired by God and thus greatly excited. Jeffrey Gitomer has written:

> *Enthusiasm is contagious. Either by presence or by absence. The more enthusiastic you are as a leader, the more enthusiastic it's likely your people will be — and the more ready and willing they will be to accept whatever task you give them.*

Geniuses tend to inspire others by their genuine enthusiasm and belief in what they are doing. When we inspire others, we tend to be motivated to keep doing our work until we reach our goal.

---

[1]Little Book of Leadership: The 12.5 Strengths of Responsible, Reliable, Remarkable Leaders that Create Results, Rewards, and Resilience

Originally, the term was used in a derogatory manner to describe someone who was so heavenly-minded that they were no earthly good. Over the years, the meaning changed to excitement and inspiration to do the job before you.

When others see how excited you are working on your project, they will become excited with you. People who become excited about what you are doing, then they will become encouragers. We all need encouragers. Get other people excited about your project and let them be your cheerleaders.

A lack of enthusiasm is often the reason for people to stop their pursuit of becoming a genius. They give up because the way is hard and they lack the zeal to continue the journey. When one is not excited about their goal, they surrender at the very least opposition.

Trust me, if you really desire to become a genius, you will face opposition. You will anger people who desire to keep you down. You will irritate people who want to think they are better and smarter than you. You will be confronted about being a "know-it-all" when your knowledge grows and you can answer many questions that others don't bother to research.

Enthusiasm will carry you through the darkest night—and you will have plenty of those. You will need enthusiasm when an attempt has failed. You will lean on enthusiasm when your strength is weak. Enthusiasm will motivate and strengthen you.

Part of being a genius is the ability to motivate others. Your enthusiasm will motivate others to assist you in your pursuit. It will motivate them to share their ideas on the subject. It will encourage them to stand behind you, even in the face of apparent failure.

Enthusiasm is energy in raw form. Harness the energy and direct it towards your goal. Use enthusiasm to your advantage. Get all excited and those around you will be excited. They will begin to do what they can to help you succeed.

I had a teacher for US History in high school who was extremely enthusiastic about history. His enthusiasm was contagious. I remember his teaching even today more than 50 years after I took his class. He was one of the influences that encouraged me to earn a master's in history. Even students who did not like history caught his enthusiasm and enjoyed, nay, looked forward to going to his class. Thank you, Coach Church.

Become excited and you will be exciting to be around and to be followed. Become engrossed in your field and you will draw others to join you.

ENTHUSIASM BREATHES LIFE INTO ANY PURSUIT!!

10 WILLINGNESS TO TAKE CHANCES

It Is Better to Try and Fail, Then to Guarantee Failure by Never Trying

Years ago, I listened to a man explain the power of the fear of failure. He said he had decided to add juggling to his list of skills. He signed up for a class in juggling. Every student was given a scarf. The teacher then told the students to stretch one of their arms out while holding the scarf. They all did as instructed. Then he shocked them all by telling them the first lesson was to drop the scarf. They were bumfuzzled. They wanted to learn how to juggle, not how to drop stuff. They already knew how to drop things.

The juggling instructor then explained, "In juggling, you will drop what you are juggling. It is inevitable. It will happen. One of the biggest obstacles to learning to juggle is the fear of dropping the ball. Now you have dropped what you were holding so you no longer need to be afraid of dropping something while you are attempting to juggle it."

A great lesson in that story. The greatest paralyzer in life is fear. FDR warned the nation during his first inaugural address (1933) that the only thing we have to fear is fear itself. The nation was at the height of the Great Depression. Fear of what might happen would keep this great nation from moving forward. FDR desired to dispel the fear and encourage courageous action to move this country forward.

Winston Churchill reminded his hearers that "Success is not final, failure is not fatal: it is the courage to continue that counts." [Sometimes this quotation is attributed to Churchill, but it seems no one can find any documentation showing he said or wrote this quotation.] Once we realize that failure is not fatal, we can be freed to try without the fear of possibly failing.

Failure is nothing more than a stepping stone to success. We need to learn how to learn and grow by and through our failures instead of being so afraid of failing we refuse to even try.

A story from my past might show how this works. Several years ago one of the shelves in one of our closets fell. I told my wife I could fix it. I had every intention of fixing it. I had the skills and know-how to fix it. I could fix it. There was one thing holding me back.

One day, my wife asked me if I was going to fix the shelf. I told her I planned to and it had only been three weeks or so. She then gently and lovingly reminded me that it had been three years not just weeks. I had to deal with reality.

I told her my problem and my delay was based on fear. I

was afraid that I would put the shelf up just half a bubble off level and she would be disappointed. She encouraged me and promised me she would not mind if the shelf was off-level, she just needed the shelf fixed. With her assurance that failure would not change her opinion of nor love for me, I was able to put my fear behind me. Within 20 minutes of this conversation, she had a new shelf installed—and it was level.

Fear of failure had kept me paralyzed. Fear of being condemned if I failed, kept me from doing something I could do. Fear is a horrible task-master. It will destroy all creativity. It will destroy all attempts to improve. It will give you a life of ho-hum at the best and most often a life full of regrets.

Those who desire to be genius must learn that fear is irrational. Well, if someone is shooting at you it is ok to fear. Fear of failure is irrational. I can guarantee you that if you attempt a great feat and fail, the world will not stop turning and life will go on.

Geniuses are not afraid to try new things. They are not bound in a box and can't get out. They thrive on adventure. A genius will never use the excuse, "I had never tried it that way before so I didn't try it ever." Geniuses look for new ways and new adventures.

You might find a genius traveling to a familiar place using new routes. They may try writing with their non-dominate hand. They will seek for and thrive on adventure. Never be afraid of change.

Be willing to take chances. Chances are steps to the goal. Try and if you don't succeed, learn from the failure and turn it into a stepping stone to success.

IF YOU DON'T TAKE CHANCES, YOU WILL NEVER KNOW IF IT WILL WORK!

11 *DYNAMIC ENERGY*

There are two types of people in this world: 1) those who wait for life to happen, and 2) those who make life happen. Become someone who does not wait for life to happen, but one who purposefully causes life to happen.

Most people fall into the first category listed. They sit around and wait their entire life then bemoan the fact they did not accomplish anything in their life. They thought that someone great would just fall into their idle life. They never tried to pro-actively cause a change in their circumstances. They never tried to change. They never tried to improve. They just waited for it to happen and were disappointed when it didn't.

Geniuses are great believers in making things happen. They set the agenda up in such a way as to accomplish their goals. They stack the deck so they will win. They are determined to go out and make things happen.

Never wait for an opportunity to come your way. Go out and find the opportunity and make things happen. Don't waste time hoping something will happen to spur you along your journey. Be pro-active. Go and create opportunities. Don't wait for the golden goose to lay you a big, fat golden egg. Go check the nest of every goose until you find the golden egg.

Geniuses spell success H-A-R-D W-O-R-K!! Many say that Thomas Alva Edison explained that genius was 2% inspiration (or genius) and 98% perspiration. Others give the credit to a lady named Kate Sanborn. It matters not who said it and what variant was spoken. The important thing to remember is that geniuses work hard to achieve what seems to come easy for them.

Don't rest on your laurels! Too many people fall short of their goals because they think a little success is enough. They feel if they accomplished something they desired; they no longer have to strive to accomplish more. They say, "Things are good enough!" A genius never thinks things are "good enough;" they strive to create more and do more. They deeply believe the time to rest is after death. Until then, they keep working to develop the better and bigger.

What if Don Shula had decided that he had done enough at Baltimore and did not try anything new at Miami? What if he decided he had enough fame and there was no need to keep pushing his team with new plays and encouraging them to play the hardest they could? Would he have ever become the winningest NFL coach? If he had waited for success to come, he would be an unknown.

When you have a deep passion for your project and are willing to work hard and long to achieve it, nothing will stand in your way. You will be willing to work hard but will do it joyfully because you know what the outcome will be. You know you will achieve your goals because you will not accept failure. Failure is no option for you. You will put in the blood, sweat, and tears to achieve your heart's desire.

When your goal is to achieve something great and you enjoy what you are doing, you will not feel like you are having to work hard. The work will be enjoyable. You may be working the hardest of anyone; but because you are working towards your passionate dream, you will feel you are having fun instead of working hard.

To work your hardest and best, you need to include taking care of your body. Eat properly, rest at least eight hours per day, and exercise enough. A healthy body adds to a healthy mind and good emotional strength.

IF YOU EXPECT TO JUST SIT AROUND AND ACHIEVE GENIUS, THEN YOU WILL NEVER ACHIEVE GENIUS STATUS!

12 ENTERPRISE

Find Steppingstones to Success in Strange Areas

B e willing to do what it takes to reach your goal. Seek opportunities to develop your genius traits. Seek models in strange and different places. Keep your eyes open for the gems that are hidden in the dirt. Be willing to do what others won't do for it is there that you might find the greatest diamond.

Geniuses are proficient at finding things where others don't think anything of value exists. Many seek to hear from God in a deep, booming voice. Moses sought God and when God revealed Himself to Moses, it was in the most unusual places.

The first encounter Moses had with God was in the middle of a desert. Moses was tending the goats and sheep of his father-in-law. That was a dirty job and considered low class. In Israel later, shepherds were considered unclean. Who would have thought God would reveal Himself to a dirty, unclean, lonely shepherd in the middle of a desert?

Moses was minding his own business when he saw

something that did not make sense. He saw a bush on fire. That, in and of itself, was not so unusual. What was unusual was that this dried-up desert scrub was ablaze but not burning up. Moses walked over to this strange bush and was even more surprised when it spoke to him. God chose to reveal Himself to Moses in a most strange way while he was doing a job many would not take at a place where many would never seek God. Read the story in the Bible in Exodus 3. God also told Moses that it did not matter that he had a speech impediment because God was going to use him.

Another strange way that God revealed Himself is found in an encounter with Elijah. Elijah is depressed. He is fleeing for his life from Queen Jezebel. Find the story in I Kings 19. God does not reveal Himself in the wind, the fire, or the earthquake. God reveals Himself to Elijah in a still, small voice.

Look for inspiration and solutions everywhere. The unknown is only unknown until you get there, then it becomes known and might hold your answer. In my humble opinion, "I don't know" should always be followed up with, "But I will find out!"

No one knows it all. There is no shame in saying you will have to look something up or do more research. Be honest but be willing to do more work.

LOOK FOR THE STEPPINGSTONES THAT ARE JUST UNDER THE WATER!

13 PERSUASION

Be the Best Cheerleader for Your Cause

Be the best motivator encouraging others to join your cause! People need encouragement to become involved in almost any project. Learn to capitalize on the fact that people have a desire to help but need a little extra nudge to become involved. Build your case and build your network.

What is the purpose of a cheerleader? To get the fans involved. Fans are sitting in the stands interacting with each other. They are watching the game and commenting to each other about the various plays. The players want to hear some noise. They want to know the fans are excited. In come the cheerleaders. They do their best to fire up the fans so they will yell for their team. They know that if the fans get excited, the players will try harder and play better.

You need to be your best cheerleader. You need to excite those around you by making great plays. In seeking to be a genius, your plays are the attempts you make to develop the skills and traits of a genius. You need to get your fans involved. You need to be excited enough that your excitement catches your fans on fire, and they cheer you on to victory.

What do most fans want? Success!! They want you to be successful so that they can say they helped you and that they know this great person who just happens to be a genius in their field of expertise. Show your fans how hard you are working. Show your fans your excitement concerning your project.

Centuries ago, a priest noticed two stonemasons who were working on building a church. One of the masons was working in a ho-hum manner. He was not really into the work, but it was his way of making money. The priest asked this worker what he was doing. The worker lazily answered, "I'm working on a church for the bishop."

The priest noticed the other mason was working hard and had a big smile on his face. So, he went over and asked why he had a smile on his face. The second mason answered, "I am building a great and glorious church for God so the people can go and worship Him with their whole heart."

Which mason would you want working for you? Of course, you would want the one with enthusiasm You want the one who sees beyond the obvious and investigates the future to see the wonderful end of the project and all it will mean.

By the way, a short time later, the new church building needed a new supervisor over the workers. Guess who the bishop appointed? The priest urged the bishop to promote the man working on a great church for God. The bishop agreed with the priest and the man who was motivated was given the job.

The enthusiastic mason had been his best cheerleader and the priest was motivated to nominate him for the new position. Be motivated in your work and your job of motivating others to help you will be much easier.

Believe in your project! In many ways, that is the easy part. The harder part is to believe in yourself! If you don't think you can do it, no one else will think you can do it. No one wants to be part of a project that is doomed to fail because the project leader is not motivated, nor does he/she believe she/he will succeed.

You have come up with a great plan and a great project. What you have dreamt about is about to become a reality. Don't sabotage yourself by doubting your abilities and goals. Be your best cheerleader and cheer others on to join your team.

YOU WON'T WIN IF YOU CAN'T MOTIVATE YOURSELF OR YOUR FANS!!

14 *OUTGOINGNESS*

E ven if a shy and timid person should reach and accomplish great things, who would know it? Shyness and timidity seldom move forward. They are afraid to call on the support they need. They are afraid to go public with their successes. They are so reclusive that others don't concern themselves with investing in their lives.

Does this mean you have to be an extrovert? No, not in any way. Natural-born extroverts indeed develop this trait easier than natural-born introverts, but being an introvert is not an automatic guarantee of doom. I have always said that God has a wonderful sense of humor. I am a natural-born introvert, but every task God has given me along my journey involves acting like an extrovert.

Have you ever heard of an introverted minister of the gospel of Jesus Christ? Neither have I. However, I am one. God has given me the ability to overcome my introvert-ness and appear like there is nothing greater than being around the masses.

When people get to know me, they are often shocked to learn that, in reality, I would prefer to not be around people and not be the center of attention. I have explained to my wife that my natural tendency is to live a quiet life. My perfect job would be to be locked in a research library alone and be able to research and write. My best friends are dead authors. They never talk back and don't judge you.

However, this is one trait that I have had to work on. I now easily say, "I don't meet strangers, just friends in the making." I can draw people around me and spend hours in different discourses. People tend to like being around me because I am an encourager.

This trait is not just being outgoing. Remember, you need cheerleaders and people to help you along the way. Therefore, you need to make friends. To make friends, you must appear friendly. You must have an inviting personality. People must see you as someone who will accept them the way they are.

Edify those around you and you will attract more followers. Your goal is to be there for others so there will be plenty of those there for you. This is not to say that you make friends to use them and demand them to follow you in return. Your desire to make people your friends must be genuine. People know if you are being friendly just to lure them into your liar to use them

Don't be a user. Be someone genuinely interested in the well-fare of others. Be concerned for their advancement. Be involved in their life. Know their family, their dreams, their goals; then set about helping them achieve their desires. Build others up.

When you build others up, you set into motion good things. You not only help them, but you reap the benefits too. Reach out to build others into the glorious edifices they can be, and you will be able to rest in their shade. Don't tear down others but encourage them to grow.

It is your job to gather supporters around you and the best way to do that is to be a supporter yourself. People love to be around others who encourage them and speak words to encouragement to them.

Realize, the larger your pool of friends, the more support and encouragement you will receive.

INVEST IN THE LIVES OF OTHERS!

15 *ABILITY TO COMMUNICATE*

Learn to Paint Word Pictures

Great orators are great word artists. Painting with oils or acrylics is simple compared to painting with words. If you desire to be a great communicator, you need to study and practice. Read the speeches of great communicators. Watch videos of speeches of great orators. Study and emulate them.

To be able to paint great word pictures, you need a mastery of words. It always baffles me when someone wants to appear to be smart, so they use big words. The problem is that they often use the words incorrectly.

I could tell you that according to psychologists the ego is very important. It is the trait that rules and controls your life. That is often called elicitation. We all need to develop our ability to allow elicitation to guide us into the fields of Elysium and thereby enjoy our life.

Sounds impressive, doesn't it. Look at those big words. Big

words don't mean a thing to a great orator unless they enhance the understanding of the subject and the meaning is known to the listeners. In the above paragraph, notice the words "elicitation" and "Elysium." Sounds like important words. Impressive! Well, when you know the meaning of those two words, the speaker goes from sounding impressive to sounding rather ignorant. "Elicitation" means the "act of drawing out emotions or facts," and "Elysium" means "the abode of the dead." Now, is that speaker sounding like someone who is intelligent?

Ronald Reagan was considered a genius when it came to politics. He knew how to organize and lead. Do you remember one of his nicknames? He often was referred to as "The Great Communicator." He knew how to use words to inspire, encourage, and change people.

Word pictures are created by using words correctly and giving descriptions that resonate with your listeners. I had a pastor that painted a good word-picture using two football teams that were vying for a place in the Super Bowl. He made the story so real that I felt as if I were in the stadium with him. However, that story meant nothing to me because I am not a football fan. Be sure your word pictures are about subjects that your listeners understand.

Jesus used agricultural word pictures because He dealt with a culture and people that were very familiar with farming. Although Jesus knew the future, He did not give an illustration using how a jet flies through the air with the ease of an eagle. They would have been completely lost with such a word picture.

Word pictures must be presented according to the

audience's life experiences. Paint pictures clearly in bold strokes. Be sure to paint a subject that your listeners can understand.

If your subject is not familiar to your listeners, be sure to break your explanation into small bites. Explain as your go along. What might be the primary level to you could be the post-graduate level to your listeners.

I remember talking with a CPA one day. He was considered brilliant by my friends and his friends. I used the term DFACS three times in explaining a matter to him. The third time I used the term, he stopped me and asked, "What is DFACS?" I thought, "This guy is supposed to be smart but has no clue what I am talking about."

I explained the term means Department of Family and Children Services. It then dawned on me that DFACS probably was not talked about much in the field of accounting. What was a common term to me, was foreign to his vocabulary.

MAKE YOUR WORD PICTURES RELEVANT AND EASY FOR YOUR LISTENERS TO IDENTIFY WITH!

16 PATIENCE

I Want Patience and I Want It Now

I f you are someone who believes in the power of prayer, let me warn you, DON'T PRAY FOR PATIENCE!! In the book of James in the Bible, James tells us:

> *2 Consider it all joy, my brethren, when you encounter various trials, 3 knowing that the testing of your faith produces endurance. 4 And let endurance have its perfect result, so that you may be perfect and complete, lacking in nothing.*
> **(James 1:2-4, NASB)**

God is telling us that when we pray for patience, He will send trials and tribulations as mentors to teach us how to wait and be patient. I prefer not to pray for more trouble to come my way.

I was taught patience by my mother as I was growing up. You see, there were five of us children in the family. I was number four. That means my older sister and my two older brothers were attended to before Mom got to me. My younger sister was last, normally. Mom was a big believer in "wait your turn."

Today's children are not taught patience like we used to be taught. We live in a generation that believes in instant gratification. No one wants to wait for anything. Fast food, drive-thru pick-ups at Lowe's, Kroger's, etc. Instant downloads of books from Amazon. Food is cooked in a fraction of time in microwaves. Instant tea and coffee. Waiting is foreign to most young people and too many of the older adults have forgotten lessons learned about waiting.

Anything worth achieving or having is well worth the time it takes to do it right. Mistakes are made in haste. Being in a constant hurry not only causes mistakes, but it is bad for our health. Just the act of being in a hurry causes stress levels to go up.

Slow Down!!

Take your time to read this next paragraph. Breathe slowly as your read it.

"It deosn't mttaer in waht oredr the ltteers in a wrod are, the olny iprmoetnt tihng is taht the frist and lsat ltteer be at the rghit pclae. The rset can be a toatl mses and you can sitll raed it wouthit porbelm. Tihs is bcuseae the huamn mnid deos not raed ervey lteter by istlef, but the wrod as a wlohe."

Even though most of the words are misspelled, you probably had no problem reading the paragraph. That is because your mind is an amazing organism. By the way, that paragraph just about gave my Grammarly program a heart attack. The purpose behind reading the above paragraph is reading something unusual naturally slows us down.

We live in a fast-paced culture. Everyone is in a hurry. We rush from one appointment to another. We don't have time to talk to anyone who is not on our busy schedule. There was a time when neighbors would sit on the porch in the cool of the evening and chat. Those days are long gone.

Learn to be patient with those who don't catch on as quickly as you do. Learn to be patient as people take their time to make up their minds. Give people permission to slow down and think through their ideas. The quality of ideas they share with you and the dedication they have after thinking before they decide to join you will greatly increase.

Put more pressure on yourself to accomplish great things than you do on anyone else. Make time to relax but stay busy.

BE EXTREMELY FLEXIBLE WITH OTHERS BUT BE DEMANDING OF YOURSELF!!

17 PERCEPTION

Notice Where Others Are Struggling, Then Act to Help Them

Notice all that is going on around you! Refuse to be narrow-minded and focus only on yourself. A genius can tend to their own needs while at the same time noticing the needs of others.

According to Maslow, before we can take care of others, we must have our own needs fulfilled. I personally disagree with this. Geniuses can be altruistic before all their personal needs are met. They have the capacity of reaching beyond their own needs to help others they see suffering. They perceive that others are struggling and need help. Their ability to see beyond today and realize they are here to help others rise along with them is amazing. They can lift others without feeling they are putting themselves down.

This perception transcends personal needs. It realizes that as one lifts others, they are setting the groundwork for their advancement. If we help others achieve, they tend to want to bring us along to continue to help and lift them. While you may be struggling, look around and find others who are struggling in the same manner. Make it your goal to help them and you will find out that helping them is helping yourself.

Helping others will often get your eyes off your problems and when you come back you will find a solution easier. Spending time away from your project to help others is not only refreshing and a cause to feel good, but it is also recharging. Reaching to those who are hurting and alleviating their pain has a way of recharging your batteries allowing you more energy to focus on your project.

Can you perceive when someone is hurting even if they say, "I'm fine"? Learn to listen behind the words. Learn to listen to pain begging for help but denying it exists. Don't live on the surface level. Dig beneath the surface to find gold, diamonds, and gems. See others for whom they are, not for whom they pretend to be.

Listen to:

https://www.youtube.com/watch?v=j4wYkS8Z3Io

We need to listen for the truth beneath the niceties.

LEARN THAT TAKING CARE OF OTHERS IS TAKING CARE OF YOURSELF!!

18 PERFECTIONISM

The Perceived Need of Perfection Has Killed Many People's Chances of Becoming a Genius

Perfectionism in moderation is needed to become a genius. I am so sorry to have to break it to you, but none of us—even geniuses—are perfect. We all have shortcomings. We all have areas of weakness.

With that said, we do need to strive to be the absolute best we can be. Don't settle for mediocrity. If you have someone near you who is satisfied with mediocrity, be a motivator for them to do better.

Geniuses never are satisfied with, "It's good enough." Always be pushing to do more, do bigger, do greater feats. Keep pushing until you reach perfection in your pursuit.

Since none of us will ever reach perfection while living on this fallen planet, reaching for perfection will be a lifelong pursuit. While you pursue perfection, don't forget to take care of yourself. Learn that to achieve your best, you have to take care of your health and your social needs. Learn to live in balance. Don't let your goals push your health and social needs to the side. Keep them in mind as you push forward. Realize that proper balance is essential to keeping yourself able to keep on keeping on.

A word about "content" as opposed to "complacent." Many confuse these two words. This results in stopping far short of the goal. Contentment is good while complacency is bad. God tells us to be content but never to be complacent.

> *But godliness with contentment is great gain. (1 Timothy 6:6)*

> *And having food and raiment let us be therewith content. (1 Timothy 6:8)*

> *10 That I may know him, and the power of his resurrection, and the fellowship of his sufferings, being made conformable unto his death; 11 If by any means I might attain unto the resurrection of the dead. 12 Not as though I had already attained, either were already perfect: but I follow after, if that I may apprehend that for which also I am apprehended of Christ Jesus. 13 Brethren, I count not myself to have apprehended: but this one thing I do, forgetting those things which are behind, and reaching forth unto those things which are before, 14 I press toward the mark for the prize of the high calling of God in Christ Jesus. (Philippians 3:10-14)*

Yes, we are to be content with what we have and how far we have come; however, we are not to stop striving to reach the goal. Keep reaching forward and one day you will be where your goal takes you.

REACH FOR PERFECTION BUT DON'T LET IT DRAG YOU DOWN!!

19 SENSE OF HUMOR

Look In the Mirror and Laugh at Yourself

Many years ago I was working very late. I was overseeing the inventory at the warehouse I was assistant manager of. I was tired. I was sleepy. I was glad when the last book was finally inventoried. Now to head home. It was around midnight when I got in my car. I cranked the motor and headed down the road. Soon I saw a line of cars headed my way. Everyone one of them had their lights on so my mind thought, "It must be a funeral." I pulled over and let the "funeral" pass. As the last car passed, it dawned on me, "It is midnight. It is dark. Of course, the cars had their lights on. It was not a funeral but just a few cars with headlights on because of the darkness." You may laugh with me because each time I remember that event, I laugh.

We all do silly stuff. Instead of being ashamed and feeling awkward, learn to laugh at our errors. My life is full of things I have done that make me shake my head and laugh. Sometimes, I do things or say things in such a way as to purposefully make others laugh. Sometimes, I just mess up and people laugh.

There are times we all need to laugh. Successful geniuses need to learn to not take themselves too seriously. When one has forgotten how to laugh, they have forgotten how to live.

In my many years of marriage counseling as a minister, I never had a couple come into my office with serious problems who remembered how to laugh. It seems that when couples forget how to laugh, they forget how to love each other. Laughter is an important ingredient in life. Laugh often.

Laughter also is a great fighter of depression. Just last night I was struggling with some depression. My best friend mentioned something to me that reminded me of a comedy sketch that Bob Newhart once did. I went to YouTube and looked it up. It is called "Stop It." It made me laugh as it always does. Then I watched several more of his comedy sketches. My laughter drove away my depression.

Some quotations on laughter:

- ➢ A good laugh heals a lot of hurts. — Madeleine L'Engle
- ➢ A smile is a curve that sets everything straight. — Phyllis Diller
- ➢ A smile is a curve that sets everything straight. — Phyllis Diller
- ➢ Against the assault of laughter, nothing can stand. — Mark Twain
- ➢ Always laugh when you can. It is cheap medicine. — Lord Byron
- ➢ From there to here, from here to there, funny things are everywhere. — Dr. Seuss

➢ I never would have made it if I could not have laughed. It lifted me momentarily out of this horrible situation, just enough to make it livable. — Viktor Frankl (This is from a survivor of the Holocaust under the Nazi regime of Hitler.)

➢ Trouble knocked at the door, but, hearing laughter, hurried away. ----- Benjamin Franklin

➢ We don't laugh because we're happy, we are happy because we laugh. ---- William James

➢ You don't stop laughing when you grow old, you grow old when you stop laughing. ---- George Bernard Shaw

As you can see, some pretty intelligent and successful people (geniuses in their own right) consider the ability to see the humor in life and yourself is mighty important. Geniuses are often high-strung and stressed. To survive, they have to see humor all around themselves including in themselves.

When you forget how to laugh, you will soon be doomed to failure no matter what you are attempting. Laughter is like a good oiling; it keeps the motor running.

WORK HARD
LAUGH MUCH
LOVE COMPLETELY
PLAY FREQUENTLY

20 *VERSATILITY*

Have you ever met a genius who works on an assembly line? One who does the same thing, the same way, day-in, and day-out? I did not think so. Geniuses are versatile individuals. Seek new adventures and new skills.

Musical geniuses tend to be able to play many different instruments. In my humble opinion, André Rieu is a musical genius. Besides music, he is also a brilliant showman and entertainer. He is a successful businessman who lives in a castle (yes, an actual castle) with his wife. He is not just a musical talent. He is so much more.

The financial geniuses of the past century were more than businessmen. They were adventurers and traveled all over this county as well as around the world. They were some of the first people to travel the roads just for adventure and vacation. They pioneered sight-seeing and were the force behind the development of motor lodges—the forerunners of motels and hotels.

Learning new and different skills and studying different fields will stimulate your mind and help you become more effective and more creative. These stimuli will help you reach new heights and come up with new ways of working on your genius traits. Never stop diversifying.

By developing new skills and learning new knowledge, you will also become more confident in your abilities. You will be more willing to try new and different ways of accomplishing your goals. I am not a seamstress, but I have learned how to tat, sew, and make clothing. My parents thought it was wise to teach their children many different life-skills. As a result, I know how to be able to do household chores, household repairs, landscaping, building, repair small machinery, and cook. I have read widely and have some knowledge on a great variety of subjects. I can carry on a conversation with those older than I am and those younger than I. Study a wide variety of subjects and learn all you can. Be a jack-of-all-trades. Be the man for all seasons.

GENIUSES TEND TO KNOW MANY SUBJECTS AND HAVE MANY DIFFERENT SKILLS

21 *ADAPTABILITY*

Those Who Fail to Adapt, Fail to Survive!

L ife changes! One of the undeniable facts of life is life changes. Life is never stagnant. Life is never the same-o-same-o. Life is fluid. Life changes from one day to the next. Sometimes, life changes from one hour to the next or even one minute to the next. Bottom line is that life is always in a state of flux. Truth never changes, but the circumstances of life are always changing. One of the signs of a genius or at least one of the traits one has to develop if they desire to become a genius is adaptability. Without adaptability, goals fail and the seeker becomes defeated.

My grandmother was born in 1899 and died in 2003. Can you imagine the number of changes she lived through? To survive in the twenty-first century, she had to adapt to myriads of changes. When she was born, the major transportation was horse and buggy. Travel was long and difficult. There were no motels or hotels to speak of. To travel from Plains, where she grew up, to Atlanta required at least one night camping out. Of course, trains existed, but most people did not ride trains unless they were going a great distance. There were no electric stoves, no refrigerators, basically no phone service, and so many of the luxuries we have come to expect did not exist. No one would hop on a plane and be in a distant city in a matter of minutes or hours. By the time she passed away, modern conveniences were abundant. Automobile travel had replaced the horse and buggy and could zip one down the highway at a break-neck speed approaching 100 mph (of course, that is faster than the speed limit, but many cars can reach that with no problem). Air travel was common. What used to take a couple of days to travel—as in from Atlanta to St. Petersburg, FL—could be done in a few hours. Yes, the list of changes could go on *ad nauseam*. To survive, she had to adapt to all these changes.

As you pursue your goal of becoming a genius, you will face changes from every area of your life. Your knowledge level will change, and you will face the challenge of adapting to properly use your new knowledge. You will need to learn how to live in harmony with those who are not as advanced in your field as you are or who do not have the working knowledge that you have. You will have to learn how to use your knowledge without seeming to be a know-it-all.

Your understanding of life and its various daily challenges will change. You will see race relations, education, interpersonal relations, and politics in a different light. You will have to learn to be more tolerant without surrendering your principles. You will have to learn how to adapt daily to the different daily issues you face. You will understand more about different cultures and how to live at peace with people who have a different cultural background than you have.

I have been reading this week a great little book (155 pages) about the people and culture of China. The book is edited by a professor in China. The text is from her Chinese students who were learning English. They write what they know about the country, the people, and the culture. What I notice is the Chinese are like the Americans—HUMAN! They have desires and wants. They have difficulties and enjoyment. What Americans have been taught about those living in China is different from what the students think about their native land.

One of the grave dangers to those who seek to develop the traits of becoming a genius is falling into the trap of "We've never done it that way before." This is a deadly trap and leads to the insanity of doing the same thing over and over yet expecting a different result. When you combine hydrogen and oxygen in a two to one proportion, you will come up with water every time. Hydrogen and oxygen combined in that proportion will never give you steel.

A simple exercise to help you see life differently is to go into the grocery store and start on the opposite end you normally start on. Items will seem out of place and look differently. You will become a little disoriented. You will see grocery shopping in a new light. You can learn to adapt to the new way of shopping, but it will take some work.

Learn to adapt to the changes and challenges you face. Change to meet the challenges. Be willing to try new ways of coping and striving.

EITHER ADAPT OR GO DOWN IN UTTER DEFEAT!!

22 *CURIOSITY*

*Curiosity May Have Killed the Cat, But the Cat Had
New Knowledge before It Died*

Curiosity is the first cousin of knowledge. Curiosity is very proud of its cousin and often is the one who introduces someone to Knowledge. If one does not have a curious nature, they will not be driven to seek new knowledge. We mentioned above how important knowledge is when one is seeking to become a genius. Since curiosity and knowledge go hand-in-hand, you must become curious about many subjects.

Your field of endeavor might be in the natural sciences. You may be seeking better ways to understand the needs of canines and how to prolong the lives of man's best friends. You might be the most brilliant zoological scientist. You may know your subject better than anyone else before you have ever known dogs. However, you need a sense of curiosity to move up to the next level.

Geniuses, as we have mentioned before, need to have a

large base of knowledge and data. You need to be widely read and have a base of knowledge in many different areas of study. You may not need to be able to change the brakes on your car, but you should have an elementary knowledge of how the brakes on a car work.

Reach out to new realms of study. Curiosity seeks to enter the world of the unknown—at least to you—and emerge with some knowledge that might one day come in handy. I have been accused of being a fountain of useless knowledge. While many of the facts I have stored in my mind may seem useless, you would not believe the number of times they have come in hand as I was working on a project.

I may not be an astronomer, but when I hear the term "black hole" my curiosity peeks. I want to know enough about what a "black hole" is to be able to keep up with a conversation between two people discussing the various interpretations of what a "black hole" is. I don't need to know all there is about "black holes," but I need enough to not appear totally uneducated on the subject.

Never be afraid to admit you do not possess certain knowledge or have certain information. No one knows it all. However, always be willing to learn what you do not know. Never be afraid to ask questions about subjects you don't fully understand. Be willing to become vulnerable so your curiosity can be sated, and your life will be enriched.

There are places where you can take college courses for free. My fields are theology, Christianity, psychology, and the like. However, I have taken courses and read books in many different fields including astronomy, biology, math, English, anthropology, and many, many more fields. Minds need constant and consistent stimulation to function at their best. Never become lazy when it comes to satisfying your curiosity.

Where are your weak areas? What subject do you not understand well? What would you like to study and know more about outside your major field? Those are things that should arouse your curiosity and cause you to seek deeper knowledge in those areas.

I have just finished reading a book that opened my eyes to many things in China. It is a book by D. M. Coffman called *China: Through the Eyes of Her Students*. The book is taken from Professor Coffman's English students' journals that she requires to be kept each term. I learned much about the culture and lives of the Chinese. I have no plans to ever go to China. I have no desire to teach about China. However, I have always been curious about different cultures and this book gave knowledge to my curiosity.

CURIOSITY IS GOD'S GIFT TO STIMULATE OUR MIND TO SEEK KNOWLEDGE!!

23 *INDIVIDUALISM*

Henry David Thoreau (1817–1862) knew the importance of individualism. He did not live his life according to the dictates of the majority of humanity. He did not follow frivolous fads. He chose the road he decided to walk. He wrote:

> *If a man does not keep pace with his companions, perhaps it is because he hears a different drummer. Let him step to the music which he hears, however measured or far away.*

Geniuses do not care that others find them odd or eccentric. They do not care if everyone else is wearing a particular brand. They do not care what the latest fashion magazine advises. He does not care what others do because he is too busy doing his own thing.

Now, one who desires to become a genius cannot disregard the dictates of the law. They cannot defy gravity and think because they don't like it, it will go away. There are many natural as well as civil laws we must obey or pay the consequences for breaking them. That is not what is being discussed here. Being an individual means doing life your way. It means living according to what is best for you and not caring if someone thinks you are odd. It means being who you are—being genuine. It means striking out on your path. It means being a trailblazer. It means being willing to walk along to reach your goals.

One of the major reasons for new products, new ways of living, new inventions, etc. not coming about is the fear of disapproval. This is different from what everyone else is doing so I won't try it. That might be the very thing that will work and change this world.

I laugh when I hear people talk about doing their own thing in their own way when they belong to a group. They are expressing their individuality by dressing in a non-conformist way. Or at least that is what they claim.

I thought it odd and thought about handing hippies a good dictionary when they talked about being unique just like all their other long-haired, blue-jean-wearing, flower-toting friends. In today's society, those who are following the Goth path think they are showing their individuality by all dressing alike in black, with facial piercing, and weird make-up. They are unique just like all their other friends.

Again, I say, "Maybe they need a good dictionary to look up the meaning of unique. You can't be unique just like all your friends." Such a misunderstanding of the term unique and individual.

Being an individual does not mean you are unique or different from everyone else. It does not mean you have to wear funny clothing and speak in a weird accent. It does not mean you forego modern conveniences or transportation. Being an individual means you are not trying to gain the approval of those around you. You do not fear their disapproval. It means you will march to the drum you hear.

Be an individual by standing for what you think is right. Be an individual by trying things in new and different ways. Reach into the unknown and make it known. Don't ask if everyone is with you; just strike out on your journey and see if anyone follows. If there are no followers, then you go on alone. If others follow, be the leader. Invite others to come, but don't let their refusal keep you from becoming one of the great ones.

ONE MAY BE THE LONELINESS NUMBER, BUT IT IS ENOUGH WHEN YOU ARE YOUR OWN PERSON!!

24 IDEALISM

Lift Your Head Higher Than the Clouds, But Keep Your Feet Planted Firmly on the Ground!

Too many people are so idealistic that they are no practical good. One of the problems with most people, when they come to idealism, is they don't seem to be able to keep it alive in the real world. One usually enters their chosen career prepared to change the world. As they spend time, they learn that most jobs involve office politics. They learn that they are not allowed to do all the great things they have dreamt of. They learn that idealism is a great mental exercise; but when it comes to practical life, it has no place.

This is especially true in the social sciences fields. Social workers, counselors, psychologists, marriage and family therapists, and the like have learned all the great theories of how to lead people out of addiction, how to cure insecurity, how to develop loving growing families, and how to live mentally healthy lives. When clients/patients don't change, they take a bite out of the idealism that the social science worker has. As time progresses, more and more chunks are removed until the bright, enthusiastic young worker start giving up on their idealism and start to believe that realism excludes idealism. Geniuses develop the ability to keep idealism alive even amid reality. When people try to rain on their parade, geniuses just bring out the umbrellas and keep on marching in their parade.

Remember that your ideal is your ideal. It is not everyone else's ideal. They may not hold to the same view of life that you do. Believe me, I have seen the underbelly of society. I have felt the sting of being ridiculed for believing that one can find good in everyone if one just looks hard enough. I have spent over 45 years seeking to change the injustices found in society and encouraging the down-trodden and outcasts of society. I have had disappointments after disappointments, but I still seek the good in all I meet.

Idealism has to do with living according to a high standard. You started on your journey believing that reaching your goal was possible. You had high and lofty ambitions. You knew you would make a splash in the pool that would cause ripples to go out into the lives of others. You knew you were out to be the best you could be and to change others along the way. You started well. What changed?

Did your abilities change? Probably not. Did the goal become unreachable? Most likely not. Did your dream change because of opposition? We discussed opposition previously: expect it and move on. What changed? Your idealism.

Take a break to restore your vision and dream. Renew your energy. Remember what it was that sparked your desire to reach your goal. Renew your commitment to your goal. Take an inventory and see what changes you have already accomplished.

Dream again! See you as your reach your goal. Think of what your goal means to you and what it can mean to others. Don't give up. Your dream is a possibility. Keep on keeping on! Keep your eyes on the prize.

DON'T LET ANYONE OR ANYTHING STEAL YOUR DREAMS!!

25 IMAGINATION

Without a Good Imagination, You Will Never Reach Your Goals

Way back in 1970, I was taking geometry in high school. The teacher gave us a problem and told us to take it home and work it out for extra credit. He also stated that it was from the national geometry teacher's magazine and the lowest number of steps it could be solved in was 31. I took that as a challenge (as I often take statements as challenges) and determined to beat 31 steps. Now according to the teacher, the best mathematical minds in the nation had solved this problem and the best of the best could do was 31 steps. Remember, I was just a high-school student, but I was determined to do better than all the experts did. I knew I solved the problem correctly, but I did it in only 30 steps. I turned my paper in the next day and the teacher looked at it and said I obviously had made a mistake.

He took it home with him that night and could not find an error. He told me the next day he was going to submit it to the organization and see if they could find my error. They could not and had to publish my work explaining that a lowly sophomore had solved the problem in fewer steps. The teacher explained that I had approached the problem backward. I had seen the problem from a different perspective. Since I had imagined the issue from a different angle, I was able to solve the problem using different steps. That is imagination.

They say that "necessity is the mother of invention;" but I say that "imagination is the mother of invention." Necessity may be the impetus, but imagination is the path. You may have a great necessity, but if you can't imagine anything different, then you are stuck where you are. Use your God-given imagination to do something great and develop something great.

When children are growing up, adults tend to squash the natural bent towards imagination. Remember as a child laying in the grass and staring up at the clouds? Did you lay there and think, "I think that is a cumulus cloud"? Did you hear thunder and think about the power of the electrical charge that caused the lightning and thunder? More than likely, you did not. If you were like most children you thought, "Wow!! The angels are bowling again!" Or maybe you thought, "Look at that bunny in the clouds."

Children use their imagination and have fun with it. As we grow, parents teach us to stop using our imagination and stick to what is real and what is true as of that time. When Da Vinci drew an object that could fly in the sky, it was not congruent with current scientific theory and especially not true to what was known at that time. He was not afraid to use his imagination and came up with many ideas way ahead of his time.

Imagination allows us to see the unseeable and hear the

unhearable. It allows us to see a different world with different inventions and methods of doing things. Imagination is the gift that allows us to ignore the nay-sayers that tell us it can't be done and hear the inner voice that assures us we can do it. Imagination sees the yet-to-be-invented as if it were already a reality.

When you look at a blank piece of paper, what do you see? Normal people will answer that question with one simple word, "Nothing." People with a little more imagination may answer, "A white piece of paper with no writing on it." However, a genius will answer more fully with something like, "I see the beginning of a great and classic novel that will take the world by storm." Imagination can see what others can't even conceive.

Those with imagination and those desiring to develop this trait need to take time to daydream. They need to think along the line of fantasy. They need to return to their childhood before they learned that some things are impossible. Geniuses are known as dreamers for a reason.

TURN YOUR DREAMS INTO REALITY!!

26 EATING YOUR ELEPHANT

How Do You Eat an Elephant?

Y ou may be thinking, "I don't want to eat an elephant." That is ok. You really don't have to eat a big, gray elephant. However, the task before you is huge. It may, and more than likely will, feel like a large elephant that is impossible to eat. It may seem like a mountain that you cannot scale. Get rid of those thoughts.

By the way, the answer to the question is "one bite at a time." This is a very important principle as you start to develop the various traits on your path to becoming a genius. You cannot do it all at one time. You have to break the elephant down into bite-size chunks. As you daily eat a little at a time, you will be amazed that you can actually eat an elephant.

Trying to change everything at once is overwhelming and one way to guarantee failure. When we try to change many things at once, we get depressed and end up giving up. We think, "I can never do all this." We think, "It is useless. I am not able to change so much."

God designed the body to change slowly. Trying to change too many things at one time harms both your physical, mental, and emotional health. You are designed for only one or two changes at a time. Too many changes at once can also lower your immunity and lead to sickness that will hamper your attempts.

Choose one or two traits at the most to work on developing at a time. Develop those until they are second nature to you. Keep practicing them even after you have mastered them. After you develop well those one or two traits then add another one or two.

Before you know it you will have developed all 24 traits. You eat your elephants one bite at a time. If you take a thousand-mile trip, you don't do the whole thousand miles in one instant. It takes time, but as you travel mile after mile you realize you are making headway and will soon be at your destination.

REMEMBER TO ENJOY THE TRIP SO YOU CAN ENJOY THE RESULTS!

27 THE PROBLEMS GENIUSES HAVE

Yes, Geniuses Have Problems Too!

Becoming a genius does not guarantee all your problems will be solved. Actually, geniuses have problems that those not so well blessed do not encounter. Because geniuses tend to think and think a lot, they tend to struggle with tasks that are too simple. Seeing what is obvious often escapes the mind of a genius.

Geniuses tend to overthink and analyze everything. Simple answers are difficult for geniuses. They intellectualize everything so that just being asked, "What is 2 + 2?" can result in a ten-minute lecture on different numbering systems. "When will you be home?" The number of answers that question engenders is staggering. You will learn there are more contingencies than you thought possible.

While most people fear failure, geniuses tend to think anything less than perfect is a failure. They think, "I made a 99 on that exam. I am such a miserable failure." If it is not going to be done perfectly, they won't even both trying. They reach for perfection and fear anything less than perfection. While some people would be elated if they just passed, geniuses feel like failures if they don't excel with perfection.

Those who are geniuses in their field have trouble relating to beginners. They tend to forget any struggle they may have had learning their field. They act like the student should understand the concepts as well as the teacher. I remember professors like that. They will spout off concepts without properly introducing them thinking everyone knows what they know. Not only do they think you should know what they know, but they don't understand why you don't know.

One of the big complaints you hear from geniuses in elementary school is that their teachers waste way too much time explaining the basics. Who needs the basics when there is advanced learning to be done?

Geniuses tend to doubt their abilities because they know how much they don't know. They are down on themselves because they don't know it all. They know their limitations and admitting they are limited is very difficult for them.

Relating to average people is difficult. Since they see deeper meanings to statements, they tend to do poorly at social events. When compliments come, they tend to struggle to understand them. For instance, the compliment, "Your hair looks nice today," becomes, "as opposed to the usual unkempt hair you usually sport." Or this one, "If I don't see you before, have a happy Thanksgiving." Does that mean if you do see them before Thanksgiving, they don't want you to have a happy Thanksgiving? Confusing!

Because dealing with the ho-hum day-to-day social interactions, geniuses tend to use rules and general guidelines. They group people into categories and see someone as belonging to this category or that category. All people in a particular category are the same. No allowances for differences. This can cause real confusion when someone breaks the mold and acts outside the boundaries of a particular category.

Geniuses find it difficult to make real friends. They often feel that non-geniuses don't understand what they mean. They feel misunderstood. Geniuses tend to speak in unconventional methods. They know what they mean but others may question them and misunderstand their intention. Geniuses may try to be friendly, but often feel they cannot be friends with those with more limited knowledge. One danger is intellectual snobbery.

Geniuses tend to have much more chronic stress and as a result, tend to sleep less. They tend to go to bed later and wake us with great ideas from their sleep all during the night. Their sleep patterns are disturbed which in turn leads to more illnesses.

Geniuses tend to be loners. They will mingle on occasion but prefer the quietness of being alone. They may be alone but are not usually lonely. They prefer jobs that allow for independence and seek the time to research. They don't necessarily research the project they are working on, but they love research for research's sake. A job where they can be alone in a research library or lab doing their own thing is perfect.

Yes, being a genius is hard work. It is something those who have not achieved the status of genius tend to seek for. However, for those who are geniuses, being a genius is both a blessing and a curse. They often long for the ability to just be average.

DO THE BEST YOU CAN TO IMPROVE YOURSELF AND BECOME A SUCCESS IN YOUR FIELD BUT BE SURE YOU CAN HANDLE THE PROBLEMS BEFORE YOU INVEST YOUR TIME AND EFFORT INTO BECOMING A GENIUS!!

DISCLAIMER: THESE TRAITS WILL HELP YOU NO MATTER WHAT YOUR STATION IN LIFE IS BUT BE SURE YOU CAN HANDLE THE UNIQUE PROBLEMS OF GENIUSES BEFORE YOU BECOME ONE. JUST BE THE BEST YOU CAN AND DEVELOPING THESE TRAITS WILL SERVE YOU WELL.

Philip van Heusen

ABOUT THE AUTHOR

Philip van Heusen is first and foremost a husband and a father. Together, his wife and he have two grown children. They are strong followers of the Lord Jesus Christ.

Philip has earned four master's degrees in four different fields: education, counseling, history, and divinity.

His greatest love is for the Lord Jesus Christ, then his family. He loves helping people grow in Christ. He loves to study then share in person and by writing with others in easy to understand language. Philip uses his education and life experiences to enlighten, encourage, and strengthen others in their relationship with the Lord Jesus Christ.

Philip desires to lead you into a relationship with the Lord Jesus Christ Who loves you and forgives you by His blood so you will know God the Father as a loving God and not a condemning God.

Be sure to check out all his other books. There are more coming soon. Below is a list of his current books and those he is already working on. Keep checking to see when new books are published, or better yet, email pvhwriting@gmail.com and asked to be informed when new books are available.

BOOKS BY PHILIP VAN HEUSEN

A Quick Look at…(Series)

The Apostles' Creed

The Foundations of Our Faith

The Lord's Prayer

Romans 12

Romans 8

Romans 5

Isaiah 6

The Fundamentals of Our Faith

The Armor of God

The Fruit of the Spirit

The Lord's High Priestly Prayer

The Doxology

Hebrews 11

Proverbs

****

Female Ancestors of Christ: Matthew 1

Becoming Genius

Working Titles for Future Books

The 16th Century: A Return to Biblical Christianity

Colonial Remnants of Charles Towne (Charleston)

Baptism

Lessons Learned from My Rose Garden

Jesus Lives Under a Bridge

It's Not Just a Man-Thing

Twentieth Century: Year by Year

Becoming Genius: The Workbook

All of Philip's books are available from Amazon in both paperback and Kindle editions.

❖ *Books in bold print are already in print at the time of this book's printing. The rest are in various stages of preparation for printing.*

Endnotes

---

[i] From merriam-webster.com/dictionary/genius retrieved on January 8, 2021.
[ii] Herman Melville, *Moby Dick*
[iii] *A Tale of Two Cities*, Charles Dickens

www.ingramcontent.com/pod-product-compliance
Lightning Source LLC
Chambersburg PA
CBHW070409220526
45467CB00001B/513